RINGING THE BELLS OF THE FUTURE

Harness the Power of Security Alarms Business in Future India!

RINGING THE BELLS OF THE FUTURE

Harness the Power of Security Alarms Business in Future India!

SAKSHAM RAJWANSHI

Worldwide Published by
Pendown Press

PENDOWN PRESS LLP
An ISO 9001 & ISO 14001 Certified Co.,
Regd. Office: 3767A, Kanhaiya Nagar,
Tri Nagar, Delhi-110035
Ph.: 8130886000, 9650072927
E-mail: info@pendownpress.com
Branch Office: 1A/2A, 20, Hari Sadan, Ansari Road,
Daryaganj, New Delhi-110002
Ph.: 011-45794768
Website: PendownPress.com

Edition: 2024
Price: ₹ 499/-
ISBN: 978-93-6338-943-4

Layout and Cover Designed by Pendown Graphics Team
Printed and Bound in India by Thomson Press India Ltd.

TABLE OF CONTENTS

Introduction i

Why This Book? ii

About The Author iv

CHAPTER - 1

Three Building Blocks of Security Alarm Business 1

- Understanding the Customer's Psychology
- Understanding the Criminal Mindset
- Growth Mindset of the Entrepreneurs

CHAPTER - 2

Product Secrets That No One Will Ever Tell You! 8

- How Indian Environment Impacts the Security Alarm Systems
- Power of Mobile Applications
- Advance Tech. Tools for Installers- When to Use and How to Make a Win-Win for All
- Different Types of Alarms
- Making a Perfect Chakravyuh

CHAPTER - 3

Let's Get to Business! 28

- What Kind of Support Does Someone Need to Thrive in The Security Industry?
- Simple Tricks for Earning More

CHAPTER - 4

Towards the bright side 45

- Getting Ready for The Future!
- What The FUTURE Holds – Forecasting & Predicting the Future of Alarms
- Simple Tricks for Earning More

What To Do Next? 47

INTRODUCTION

To win great battles, you need an army with the right skills and the right weapons.

I thought we had whatever it takes to win the game of business, but I was wrong.

My love for learning has proven to me that the game keeps on changing. In a world that is changing so dynamically, the only constant is CHANGE.

Great writers, philosophers and both great women and men have always claimed that if one changes with time, they will always have 'time' by their side.

A well-planned security business strategy can do wonders in your business, irrespective of the industry you're in, provided it is put together in a seamless and cohesive manner.

Trust me, I speak from experience.

WHY THIS BOOK?

Hello, my name is Saksham Rajwanshi. I am a security alarm specialist.

My tryst with security and surveillance began early in my career as a security professional, nine years back. Ever since then, it has never failed to impress me in terms of establishing lasting relationships with my clients but also in terms of generating value for them.

I live and breathe security and surveillance solutions daily, and it continues to top my list of offerings in my business.

Over the years, I've successfully used these selling techniques to grow my family business and have helped numerous CCTV system integrators and entrepreneurs get more from their security solution-related initiatives.

The journey so far has been brilliant!

You might be wondering why I'm sharing this free book when I could have charged a premium for sharing the information. After all, if you implement the suggestions contained within this book, you can make a real killing and grow your business in leaps and bounds.

Besides, as we often hear in business parlance, "there is no free lunch".

So why this free book?

One, being in love with Security Alarms and CCTV Surveillance, it breaks my heart to not harness the power of

Security Alarms. So, I want to put as many people as possible on the right path.

Two, I am unable to coach everyone personally due to time constraints, so this book is a gift to system integrators and installers that shares over 15 valuable lessons that I have learned during my journey as a reliable security professional.

I hope these lessons will steer you to the path of success in your business. So, without further ado, let's explore the 15 lessons I learned about the security alarm business.

Your friendly security specialist, Saksham Rajwanshi

About Author

Since the beginning of my conscious life, I have been surrounded by technology, fascinated by the man-made miracles and what they can offer to mankind. I filed my first research paper related to how wonderful light and sound can be, if put together.

As an entrepreneur with a passion for technology, I went ahead to learn automation using technology from an amazing business automation coach, who helped me develop the 'service lite' framework, which automates complex business tasks to bring the business to auto pilot.

This award-winning system is currently being used by over 400 of our workforces, most of whom are in the field to make our company the best 'system integrator of the year' by BFSI Industry.

It is a pride to share with you that we have been transforming the security alarm industry since 1981 with MAKE IN INDIA, 34 years before anyone even thought of it.

I will take a minute to share the idea behind Digitals... It was the '70s, and India was struggling to establish itself as a growing nation. Business automation was the need of the hour. The first product was the token display, which simply displayed the token number, making queue management effective at bank branches and thereby solving the complex issue of calling out token numbers, creating confusion and chaos at the branches.

The journey from a token display machine to highly advanced IP-based alarm panels has been quite fascinating.

Evolving over time, our company pioneered many great technologies, from bringing the first lot of DVR-Cards to North India to introducing Metal Detectors to the Indian Aviation Industry.

Over the years, there has only been a constant zeal for sharing amazing technologies with our society.

Our panels have been designed to work in the harshest environments, from Jammu Kashmir's lowest temperatures to Kerala's lightning affairs.

Blessed to be able to train security professionals across top Government Organisations, I have become a popular choice for training on advancements in technologies in Government and Private institutions across the country.

CHAPTER 1

Three Building Blocks of Security Alarm Business

Understanding the Customer's Psychology

It will really be very powerful for some and overwhelming for others, but the question to ask is:

What is my customer thinking?

What are they thinking, when...

- They wake up
- They plan a vacation
- They are Happy
- They are Sad
- They want to buy something
- They think about us

If we can feel our customer, it will become fairly simple to identify something simple... How do I make my potential lead buy my product or service?

Let me share my understanding of the general psychology of any customer while choosing or purchasing any product or service:

- **Needs & Desires:** This is the first but ultimate aspect. Customers always buy anything that fulfills their needs or desires. Understanding whether it is solving a problem, satisfying a want, or simply enhancing their lifestyle is very crucial.
- **Emotion:** The second most important aspect during the decision-making process is their emotion. That excitement, comfort, security, or status.
- **Perception of value:** This is a really deep aspect as it differs from person to person, location to location but plays a critical role in purchase decisions. We will expand on this aspect throughout this book to create the perception of value addition, which you are offering to your clients.

There are many other aspects, but since this book is about security alarms, we will keep it short to give you an overview and provide you with insight into what works and how it works while building trust and credibility with our clients.

Understanding the Criminal Mindset

Just like any business, we have to understand the most basic – atomic level reason for what Job our Product or Service does for our clients.

But to understand this, in this case, we have to understand what job the prime suspect or the criminal has to do. While this may sound totally off-topic, it is important to know the threat so we can be good at solving it through our solution.

Let us look at how and why criminals commit crime in our industry:

- **Exploiting Vulnerabilities:** Criminals might look for weaknesses in security systems, such as outdated technology or poorly maintained equipment, to exploit for their gain.
- **Knowledge of Systems:** Some criminals may have in-depth knowledge of security systems, allowing them to bypass or disable alarms without detection.
- **Profit Motive:** Financial gain is often a primary motivator for criminal activity. This could involve stealing valuable items from properties with weak security or selling information about vulnerabilities to other criminals.
- **Risk Assessment:** Criminals might assess the risks associated with breaking into properties with security alarms and develop strategies to minimize the likelihood of getting caught.
- **Adaptability:** Criminals may adapt their tactics based on changes in technology or security measures, constantly

seeking new ways to bypass security systems and gain access to properties.

- **Insider Threats:** In some cases, individuals within the security alarm industry or members of the premises being guarded may exploit their access and knowledge for criminal purposes, such as providing information about security system vulnerabilities to criminals.

We have covered the primary concerns; there are many other socio-economic, geographic, and emotional reasons for committing crimes, which we will cover later.

Let me make you understand this through an example: Imagine that you are at a luxury villa, and upon asking the owners/nearby people how burglars commit burglaries, you get info that they typically break the glass windows to break in... knowing that criminals choose the easy way and break in at night will give you better insight for you to design a solution that will actually do its job for the customer.

GROWTH MINDSET OF THE ENTREPRENEURS

As entrepreneurs, we often feel lonely at the top. Little missed opportunities and losses make us fall into a pit from where we often do not want to come out.

Once in that vicious circle, we complicate things that are not as complicated.

Remember, we chose business for freedom, happiness, and financial security... but with some unpleasant experiences, we often build a boundary wall so big that not even our family, our staff, or our customers can enter our hearts, restricting our growth and blocking abundance!

- As entrepreneurs with a growth mindset, challenges are seen as opportunities for learning and growth rather than obstacles.
- They persevere in the face of setbacks and failures, viewing them as learning experiences rather than reasons to give up, actively seeking feedback and constructive criticism to improve themselves and their ventures.
- Such amazing entrepreneurs believe that effort and hard work are essential for success, and they bounce back from setbacks with renewed determination.

And most importantly, they are inspired by others' achievements and see them as sources of learning and motivation rather than threats or sources of envy.

I challenge you to break free from the trap and enter the world of abundance by using some tricks:

1. When you are Fearful or Depressed - Laugh Out Loud

Find the reason that is stopping you and laugh over it!

Do it alone, do it in a park, do it with your family, do it with your friends...

Laughing puts us in a state of not knowing. It shifts focus from the problem to the simple act of laughing.

Laughing at your fear, laugh at yourself for thinking about that fear, or laugh at others who are living life with fear... just laugh!

2. Judger/Learner Mindset

Often, we become judgmental of our being, of everything that is happening around us, and of everyone around us.

This way, we forget the learner inside us who has to constantly keep on learning from everything, everyone, and every situation that is happening right in front of our eyes.

Life is a learning journey; we start learning from inside a mother's womb and keep on learning, learning and learning until the learning stops (and so does our heartbeat).

It is easy to shift from JUDGER TO LEARNER mode by simply becoming conscious and asking, "Why am I being judgmental?" and then, "What can I do to simply learn about how to ......"

It might seem very difficult, but changing your questions can really change the world around you in your favor.

Be it asking for payments from a client or simply suggesting a good movie, ask yourself, “What can I do to convince the person to understand?”.

CHAPTER 2

Product Secrets That No One Will Ever Tell You!

How Indian Environment Impacts the Security Alarm Systems

The Indian environment can significantly affect the working of a security alarm system due to various factors such as climate, power supply, infrastructure, and cultural considerations.

- **Climate:** India experiences diverse climatic conditions ranging from extreme heat in some regions to heavy monsoon rains and humidity in others. Security alarm systems must be designed to withstand these conditions to ensure reliable operation.
- **Power Supply Reliability:** Power outages and fluctuations are common in many parts of India. Security alarms need to have backup power sources such as batteries or generators to ensure continuous operation during power failures.
- **Infrastructure Challenges:** In some areas, challenges such as poor road conditions or limited internet connectivity may impact the installation and functioning of security alarm systems. Installers need to adapt to these challenges and implement appropriate solutions.

- **Cultural Considerations:** Cultural factors may also influence the design and implementation of security alarms.

For example, in densely populated areas, false alarms may be more common due to factors like stray animals or noisy environments. Alarm systems should be designed to minimize false alarms while still providing effective security.

India faces various security threats ranging from petty theft to more serious crimes such as burglary or vandalism.

Security alarm systems need to be tailored to address these specific threats and provide adequate protection to homes, businesses, and other properties.

Environmental Condition	Consideration	Points/ Remarks
Weather Conditions	Resistance to rain, snow, and extreme temperatures	
	Ability to function in high humidity environments	
Location	Indoor or outdoor installation	
	Compatibility with mounting surfaces	
Power Source	Battery-powered or wired	

	Backup power options	
Connectivity	Wi-Fi, cellular, or landline connectivity	
	Compatibility with smart home systems	
Detection Range	Coverage area and range of motion detection	
	Ability to adjust sensitivity	
False Alarm Prevention	Pet-friendly settings	
	Advanced detection algorithms	
Integration	Compatibility with existing security systems	
	Remote monitoring and control options	

POWER OF MOBILE APPLICATIONS

Keeping in view the external factors, there will be times when the alarm will ring at night due to some external reasons - like loud sound at nearby parties, power fluctuations, lightning, etc. While any system could only reduce the occurrence of alarms in these situations, they cannot be ruled out completely as the system is merely a machine working on inputs.

In order to save us from the nuisance, we must have a backup plan. This backup plan is also required to fetch the actual reason for the alarm, take the right measures, and, in fact, even redo everything which the client wants, when they want.

The answer to this complex problem is very simple: a Mobile Application or Mobile Control.

The Mobile Application helps users gain the following benefits:

1. **Remote Control:** Users can arm, disarm, and monitor their security system from anywhere with or without an internet connection, providing peace of mind and convenience.
2. **Real-time Notifications:** Receive instant alerts on your smartphone for any security breaches or events detected by the alarm system, enabling quick response.
3. **Customization:** Adjust alarm settings, notification preferences, and user permissions directly from the mobile app, tailoring the system to individual needs.

4. **Integration with Smart Devices:** Seamlessly integrate the security alarm with other smart home devices and systems, such as lights, locks, and thermostats, for enhanced automation and control.

5. **Historical Data and Reports:** Access historical data and activity logs through the app, allowing users to review past events and analyze trends for improved security management.Multi-user Access: Grant access to multiple users with their own login credentials, enabling family members or trusted individuals to monitor and control the security system.

6. **Emergency Response Coordination:** Directly contact emergency services or designated contacts in case of an alarm activation through the app, facilitating quick and coordinated response.

7. **Software Updates and Enhancements:** Receive software updates and new features directly through the mobile app, ensuring the security system stays up-to-date with the latest advancements and improvements.

As an installer or solution provider, it is very important that we share these aspects with our clients so they are able to get the benefits of the mobile application, enhancing their user experience and making it easy for them to use the solution which you have proposed.

Advance Tech. Tools for Installers- When to Use and How to Make a Win-Win for All

Often, we come across a question from seasoned System Integrators: why do they need a mobile app, especially when their team is trained enough to set up any alarm systems with ease.

But we believe it is important to understand the real usage of Mobile Apps for security alarm OEMs and how to make it a win-win for all stakeholders.

Let us review the top benefits one can get from a mobile application designed for the system integrators:

1. **Remote Configuration:** System integrators can remotely configure and customize security alarm systems using the mobile app, eliminating the need for on-site visit, speeding up installation and setup processes.
2. **Real-time Monitoring:** Monitor the status of security alarm systems in real-time through the mobile app, allowing system integrators to identify and address issues promptly, minimizing downtime and ensuring optimal performance.
3. **Diagnostic Tools:** Access diagnostic tools and troubleshooting guides through the mobile app to diagnose and resolve technical issues quickly and efficiently, reducing the need for costly service calls and onsite visits.
4. **Firmware Updates:** Receive notifications and perform firmware updates for security alarm components remotely via the mobile app, ensuring that systems are always up-to-date with the latest security patches and enhancements.

5. **Documentation Access:** Access technical documentation, user manuals, wiring diagrams, and installation guides through the mobile app, providing system integrators with essential resources and reference materials while on-site.

6. **Training Resources:** Provide training materials, instructional videos, and certification programs through the mobile app to support ongoing training and professional development for system integrators.

7. **Customer Support:** Access customer support resources, contact technical support representatives, and initiate support tickets directly from the mobile app, enabling system integrators to resolve customer issues quickly and efficiently.

8. **Project Management:** Manage security alarm installation projects, track project progress, and communicate with team members and customers through the mobile app, streamlining project management processes and improving collaboration.

9. **Inventory Management:** Manage inventory levels, track equipment usage, and create purchase orders for security alarm components directly from the mobile app, simplifying inventory management and ensuring that necessary equipment is available when needed.

10. **Enhanced Efficiency and Productivity:** By providing access to essential tools, resources, and support services through a mobile app, system integrators can improve efficiency, productivity, and overall customer satisfaction.

While not all but many caring security alarm manufacturers offer this service, it is vital that you decide if your business really wants the help at your palms when you need it or you can manage things on your own.

This reminds me of a small story when one of our partner's technicians (or Field Associates, as they like to refer to them) was on one of the client's sites and the clients wanted the settings to be configurable on their mobile. The poor fellow did not know anything about the Mobile Application settings. But the savior training video section of our company had everything he needed, just in the right sequence, which got him to be able to not only configure the customer's mobile application but also educate them about the features and know-how of the app.

Different Types of Alarms

A. Categorization on The Basis of The EN Grades

The EN Grades refer to the European standards for intruder alarm systems, specifically outlined in the European Norm (EN) standards EN 50131 series. These standards categorize intruder alarm systems based on their grades, which are indicative of the system's level of security and reliability. The grades range from Grade 1 to Grade 4, with Grade 1 being the lowest and Grade 4 being the highest. Here's a brief overview of the different types of alarms based on the EN Grades:

1. **Grade 1: Low Security**
   - Typically used in low-risk environments where the threat level is minimal
   - Basic protection against opportunistic intruders
   - Suitable for residential applications with a low risk of intrusion
2. **Grade 2: Low to Medium Security**
   - Suitable for residential and commercial properties with a moderate risk of intrusion
   - Offers a higher level of security compared to Grade 1.
   - May include additional features such as tamper protection.
3. **Grade 3: Medium to High Security**
   - Suitable for commercial and industrial properties with a significant risk of intrusion
   - Provides a higher level of security and reliability compared to Grade 2

- May include features like dual-path communication and advanced tamper protection

4. **Grade 4: High Security**

Designed for high-security applications such as banks, jewellery stores, or critical infrastructure.

- Offers the highest level of security and reliability.
- Includes advanced features like redundant communication paths, high-level tamper protection, and more.

Each grade comes with specific requirements for various components of the alarm system, such as control panels, detectors, signaling devices, and communication methods. It's important to choose an alarm system that aligns with the security needs of the specific environment in which it will be installed. Additionally, compliance with the relevant EN Grade standards ensures that the alarm system meets certain quality and performance criteria.

Being a part of LITD 26 (The BIS Committee working on the standards for Security Alarms - Intrusion Alarms) has given me the privilege to share our insights towards making of the Indian standard for security alarms (often called as Intrusion Alarms). It has been a pleasure to learn from the entire team of LITD 26.

B. Categorization on The Basis of The Communication Technologies

Out of the many ways to categorize the different types of security alarms, identifying the methods used for transmitting signals and information between different components of the system is another approach. Various communication technologies are employed to ensure the reliability and effectiveness of these systems. Here are different categorizations based on communication technologies:

1. **Wired Communication Systems**
   - **Powerline Communication:** This method utilizes the electrical wiring in a building for communication. It can be used for transmitting signals between components and is one of the simplest or perhaps the oldest methods for communication in a local setup.
   - **Landline (PSTN):** Traditional phone lines are used for communication between the alarm system components and the owners/stakeholders or the central monitoring station. This method is reliable but vulnerable to line cuts.
   - **Ethernet:** Security systems can use standard Ethernet cables for communication. This method provides a stable connection but may be susceptible to physical tampering.
2. **Wireless Communication Systems**
   - **Wi-Fi:** Alarm components communicate through Wi-Fi networks. This method offers flexibility

but may be vulnerable to signal interference and hacking.

- **Cellular (GSM/GPRS/3G/4G/5G):** Security systems can transmit signals using cellular networks, providing a reliable wireless connection. It is less susceptible to physical tampering compared to landlines.
- **Satellite Communication:** In remote areas or for critical infrastructure, satellite communication may be employed to ensure connectivity in areas where traditional communication methods are unreliable or unavailable. These are hard to find but exclusively designed for mission critical applications.

C. Categorization on The Basis of The Industry

Just like we have different clothes, gear, and seasons, we have different alarms based on their usage or application. Depending on the industry where they are going to be installed, the follow categorization can be observed:

1. **Residential Security Systems**
    - Designed for homes and private residences.
    - Focus on protecting residents and property from unauthorized access and burglary.
    - Typically includes door/window sensors, motion detectors, and sometimes integrates video surveillance.
2. **Commercial and Business Security Systems**
    - Aimed at securing commercial properties, businesses, and offices.

- Can include Security Alarm systems integrated with access control systems, surveillance cameras.
- May have features like keycard access, monitoring for unauthorized entry, and integration with fire alarm systems.

3. **Retail Security Systems**
    - Tailored for retail establishments.
    - Focus on preventing theft, shoplifting, and ensuring the safety of customers and staff.
    - May include Security Alarm System security cameras integrated with EAS (Electronic Article Surveillance) systems, video surveillance, and point-of-sale integration.
4. **Industrial and Manufacturing Security Systems**
    - Customized for the security needs of industrial facilities and manufacturing plants.
    - This involves a security alarm system integrated with access control for restricted areas, surveillance of critical infrastructure, and fire alarms.
5. **Banking and Financial Security Systems**
    - Designed for the unique security requirements of banks and financial institutions.
    - May include an advanced security alarm system with integrated or standalone access control, vault security time locks, video surveillance, and a fire alarm system.
    - Compliance with regulatory standards is crucial in this sector.

6. **Healthcare Security Systems**
   - Tailored for hospitals, clinics, and healthcare facilities.
   - Focus on protecting patient information, restricting access to sensitive areas, and ensuring the safety of patients and staff.
   - This involves a security alarm system integrated with access control for restricted areas, a nurse calling system, surveillance of critical infrastructure, and fire alarms.
7. **Educational Institution Security Systems**
   - Designed for schools, colleges, and universities.
   - Aimed at preventing unauthorized access, ensuring student safety, and addressing emergency situations.
   - May include a security alarm system integrated with access control, video surveillance, and fire alarms.
8. **Government and Public Sector Security Systems**
   - Developed to meet the security needs of government buildings and public infrastructure.
   - Often involves high-security measures, security alarm systems with access control, and integration with other government systems.

9. **Critical Infrastructure Security Systems**
    - Tailored for protecting critical infrastructure such as power plants, water treatment facilities, and transportation hubs.
    - It involves robust security measures, a security alarm system, and often includes redundancy for critical components.
10. **Smart City Security Systems**
    - Aimed at enhancing the security and safety of urban areas through the integration of various technologies.
    - It involves surveillance, access control, security alarm systems, and data analytics for comprehensive security management.

While all the above systems can work as standalone systems or be integrated with each other to relay information to the owner/user, they can also be connected to the Central Monitoring Station (either self-operated or outsourced), making the security arrangements stronger.

It is therefore the need of the hour to understand the risk and the outcome the clients want to achieve with the system. This understanding will help any system designer and integrator in designing a system so robust that not even a bird can flap its feathers without getting noticed.

This brings us to the next and very important aspect, which I believe is very important to learn by heart for any security system designer and integrator.

Making a Perfect Chakravyuh

"Chakravyuh" is a term with its roots in ancient Indian epic literature, specifically in the Hindu epic Mahabharata. It refers to a military formation, often described as a circular or labyrinthine arrangement of soldiers, which is challenging to penetrate or escape from. It is a strategic formation used in warfare to create a defensive and formidable structure.

The most famous reference to the Chakravyuh is found in the Mahabharata during the battle of Kurukshetra. Abhimanyu, the son of Arjuna, knew how to enter the Chakravyuh but not how to exit it, as he had only partially heard the military strategy while in his mother's womb. Despite his heroic efforts, Abhimanyu was eventually overwhelmed and met his fate within the Chakravyuh.

Metaphorically, "Chakravyuh" is sometimes used in modern contexts to describe a complex or intricate situation, system, or problem that is difficult to navigate or escape, drawing from the concept of the military formation in the ancient Indian epic.

In modern days, it can be linked to a security alarm system guarding any valuable asset or important area in any premises. This involves implementing multiple layers of security measures to create a defense that is difficult to penetrate. Let us understand how we can develop a 'chakravyuh' in any system:

1. Identify the primary asset (for simplicity, we will refer to any object, area, or person as the 'primary asset').

2. Identify the points of entrances into the premises where the Primary Asset is located.
3. Identify the physical routes, passages, or walkways between the entrance(s) and the Primary Asset.
4. Calculate the number of Doors & Windows between the starting and endpoints.

Now, here is the basic strategy to enhance the security of an asset using a multi-layered approach:

1. **Perimeter Security**
   - Implement physical barriers and deterrents around the asset, such as fences, walls, and access control points.
   - Use sensors like infrared detectors or motion sensors to monitor the perimeter and detect any unauthorized movements.
2. **Access Control**
   - Employ access control systems to regulate entry to the asset.
   - Use electronic key cards, biometric authentication, or PIN codes to restrict access to authorized personnel only and alarm in case of attempts at unauthorized access.
3. **Surveillance Cameras**
   - Install a comprehensive network of surveillance cameras to monitor key areas both inside and outside the asset.
   - Use high-resolution cameras with night vision capabilities for 24/7 monitoring.

4. **Security Alarm System**
    - Deploy a security alarm system that includes sensors on doors, windows, and other potential entry points. Also, deploy motion sensors, vibration sensors, light sensors, and tilt sensors as per the size, location, and nature of the primary asset.
    - Integrate the system with alarms that activate when unauthorized access is detected.
5. **Alarm System Integration**
    - Depending on the client's budget and the value or criticality of the primary asset, implement a centralized alarm system that integrates various sensors and detectors.
    - Configure the alarm system to provide real-time alerts to security personnel or a monitoring center.
6. **Dual-Path Communication**
    - Ensure that the alarm system has redundant communication paths, such as both landline and cellular connections.
    - Redundancy helps maintain communication even if one path is compromised.
7. **Physical Security Measures**
    - Consider physical deterrents within the asset, such as safes or vaults for valuable items such objects in front of or near the asset so it is not easily accessible.
    - Implement tamper-resistant features on critical equipment.

8. **Security Personnel**
   - Employ trained security personnel to monitor and respond to security alerts.
   - Implement access control measures for security personnel to ensure accountability.
9. **Regular Security Audits**
   - Conduct regular security audits and assessments to identify vulnerabilities and areas for improvement.
   - Update security protocols based on audit findings.
10. **Emergency Response Plan**
    - Develop and regularly rehearse an emergency response plan that outlines actions to be taken in case of a security breach.
    - Ensure coordination with local law enforcement if required.

Creating a "Chakravyuh" in a security alarm system involves combining various security measures to create a comprehensive and layered defense. It's essential to continually evaluate and update security protocols to adapt to evolving threats and vulnerabilities. If you are an end user, consulting with security experts or professionals can also provide valuable insights into tailoring security measures based on the specific characteristics and risks associated with the asset being protected.

However, it works for you, believe me, learning from history makes it easier for us to design the system. A classic Palace Security and Intruder Detection where rulers often incorporated security features such as guarded entrances, secret passages, and mechanisms to detect intruders. If you have ever been to Lucknow, the famous Imambara in Lucknow (built by Nawab Asaf-ud-Daula, the Nawab of Awadh, in 1784), you must have experienced one of the notable features which is the Bhool Bhulaiya, a labyrinthine network of narrow passages. With really amazing tricks such as whispering through the walls and identical-looking passages, even if a thief/intruder comes inside the premises, he surely would have lost their way and been caught easily. Without the electronic alarms, these measures were designed to prevent unauthorized access.

CHAPTER 3

Let's Get to Business!

What Kind of Support Does Someone Need to Thrive in The Security Industry?

Our success has been based on partnerships from the very beginning. - Bill Gates

In nature, symbiosis refers to a close and often long-term interaction between two different species. This interaction can be mutually beneficial (mutualism), beneficial for one species and neutral for the other (commensalism), or beneficial for one species while harming the other (parasitism).

As an entrepreneur, it is our job to create win-win situations in every partnership if we are to succeed together, maintaining mutualism, some commensalism, and avoiding parasitism.

Now, let us dive deep into the support we will require from product/solution manufacturers to create a win-win situation for all:

System integrators often rely on manufacturers for technical support when implementing security alarm systems. Here are some common types of support manufacturers may offer:

1. **Product Training:** Manufacturers can provide training sessions for system integrators to familiarize them with the features, installation processes, and troubleshooting methods for their security alarm systems.

2. **Technical Documentation:** Manufacturers typically provide detailed technical documentation, including user manuals, installation guides, and troubleshooting guides, to assist integrators in understanding and implementing their products correctly.

3. **Pre-Sales Support:** Manufacturers may offer pre-sales support to help integrators select the right products for their specific project requirements. This can involve consultations, product demonstrations, and recommendations.

4. **Post-Sales Support:** After the sale, manufacturers often provide ongoing technical support to help integrators with installation issues, configuration problems, and any other challenges they encounter during the implementation process.

5. **Software Updates and Patches:** Manufacturers regularly release software updates and patches to improve the functionality, performance, and security of their alarm systems. Integrators can typically access these updates through manufacturer support channels.

6. **Troubleshooting Assistance:** Manufacturers usually have technical support teams available to assist integrators with troubleshooting issues that arise during installation or operation. This can involve phone support, email support, or online chat support.

7. **Warranty Support:** If any components of the alarm system are found to be defective or malfunctioning, manufacturers typically offer warranty support to replace or repair the affected components.

8. **Customization Support:** In some cases, manufacturers may provide customization support to help integrators tailor the alarm system to meet specific customer requirements or integrate it with other systems.

In addition to this, we have found it really helpful for our system integrators to be able to manage all content in one place, assign training, and issue certificates for the training programs of our systems through our Training Management System. Also, the free mobile app and Health Monitoring/ Remote Diagnostic setup on almost all systems enable them to save 10-12K monthly by remotely resolving issues.

With the right kind of business partner, you are bound to be successful!

Simple Tricks for Earning More

A. Inventory Management

I believe that business is similar to artwork. The more brushes, strokes, techniques, and styles you know, the better you are at creating a masterpiece. While it is the most dreaded aspect of every business, it is often neglected by any business owners.

Tweaking and applying amazing techniques of SCM (Supply Chain Management) can unlock a huge chunk of cash flow. Let us understand this through the experience of my friends Dhruv and Ankur.

My friend Dhruv owns a textile shop in Old Delhi. They had always struggled with managing their inventory of silk sarees, often ending up with excess stock that took up valuable space and tied up their capital. One day, while attending a training program, Dhruv heard about the concept of Just-In-Time (JIT) inventory management. Inspired by the idea, he decided to give it a try.

Dhruv and his brother Ankur began by analyzing their sales data and customer preferences more closely. They noticed that certain types of sarees were consistently in high demand during specific festivals and wedding seasons. Armed with this knowledge, they adjusted their ordering patterns to match the actual demand, rather than relying on gut feelings or traditional ordering schedules.

Instead of stocking up on large quantities of sarees in anticipation of future demand, Dhruv and his family started ordering smaller, more frequent shipments from their suppliers. They made sure to place orders just in time to meet the immediate needs of their customers, reducing the amount of excess inventory they had to store.

To ensure their suppliers could keep up with this new JIT ordering system, Dhruv and Ankur communicated regularly and built strong relationships with them. They shared their sales forecasts and kept them informed about any changes in demand patterns, allowing the suppliers to adjust their production schedules accordingly.

As a result of implementing JIT inventory management, they saw significant improvements in their business. They no longer had to deal with the burden of excess inventory taking up space in their shop. Their capital was freed up, allowing them to invest in other areas of their business, such as marketing and expanding their product range.

While the textile or fashion industry enjoys other benefits of SCM, it can be applied in any field, including ours.

Using simple and logical techniques, any business owner can unlock their cash flow, which is often stuck in inventory and later becomes obsolete. Let us take a look at these principles:

1. **Demand Forecasting and Planning**

   The first & foremost step is to use accurate demand forecasting techniques to predict future demand patterns. By understanding demand variability and trends, you can optimize inventory levels to meet customer needs while avoiding overstocking.

   I remember when we provided the first inventory management software to one of our clients in Noida, which helped them manage not just Security Alarms but also all other products. This helped them anticipate demand fluctuations influenced by different Months.

2. **Just-In-Time (JIT) Inventory**

   Implement JIT principles to minimize inventory holding costs and reduce waste. By synchronizing purchase with demand, you can minimize the need for excess inventory storage.

3. **Vendor-Managed Inventory (VMI)**

   Collaborate closely with suppliers to manage inventory levels more efficiently. VMI allows suppliers to monitor inventory levels and replenish stock automatically, reducing the need for large buffer stocks.

4. **Safety Stock Optimization**

   Use statistical methods to determine optimal safety stock levels based on demand variability, lead times, and service level requirements. This ensures adequate inventory availability while minimizing excess inventory.

5. **ABC Analysis**

   Classify inventory items based on their value and importance. Focus on optimizing inventory management for high-value items (A-items) while adopting more relaxed policies for low-value items (C-items).

6. **Batch Size Optimization**

   Reduce order quantities and batch sizes to minimize inventory holding costs and improve inventory turnover. This can be achieved through economies of scale, installation flexibility and process optimization.

7. **Lead Time Reduction**

   Shorten lead times by improving supplier relationships, streamlining transportation and logistics processes, and implementing lean principles. This can help reduce the need for large safety stocks.

8. **Inventory Centralization and Pooling**

   Consolidate inventory in centralized locations or shared pools to achieve economies of scale and reduce overall inventory levels. This approach is particularly effective for products with sporadic demand or long lead times.

9. **Continuous Improvement**

   Implement a culture of continuous improvement to identify and eliminate inefficiencies in inventory management processes. Regularly review and optimise inventory policies, processes, and technologies to drive ongoing reductions in inventory levels.

10. **Technology Adoption**

    Leverage advanced supply chain technologies such as inventory optimization software, demand planning tools, and real-time visibility solutions to improve inventory management accuracy, efficiency, and responsiveness.

When I was pursuing my B. Tech, I had the opportunity to take Supply Chain Management as one of my minors. Little did I know that SCM is a world in itself. From milk runs to delivery centers and from JIT to inventory turn management, there is so much that a business owner must be aware of to manage their business effectively.

If you have any questions about how you can leverage SCM principles and would like to know more, I will be sharing the details with you towards the end of this book. Till then, keep reading and making notes on:

HOW CAN I IMPLEMENT THIS IN MY BUSINESS?

b. Automation And How to Achieve It

The history of business automation can be traced back to the early 20th century, with the advent of mechanical and electromechanical systems designed to automate repetitive tasks in manufacturing and administrative processes.

1. **Industrial Revolution:** The Industrial Revolution of the 18th and 19th centuries marked the beginning of widespread automation in manufacturing.

   Innovations such as the steam engine, mechanized looms, and assembly lines revolutionized production processes, leading to increased efficiency and productivity.

2. **Early Computing Devices:** In the mid-20th century, the development of early computing devices laid the groundwork for modern business automation.

   Machines like the tabulating machines developed by Herman Hollerith in the late 1800s and the first electronic computers like the ENIAC (Electronic Numerical Integrator and Computer) in the 1940s began to automate tasks such as data processing and calculations.

3. **Mainframe Computers:** In the 1950s and 1960s, mainframe computers became more widely available and affordable for businesses.

   These large, centralized computers were used for tasks such as payroll processing, inventory management, and financial calculations, streamlining administrative operations and improving accuracy.

4. **Emergence of Software:** The 1970s and 1980s saw the emergence of software applications designed specifically for business automation.

   Early enterprise resource planning (ERP) systems, such as MRP (Material Requirements Planning) and MRP II (Manufacturing Resource Planning), helped businesses manage their production processes, inventory, and supply chains more efficiently.

5. **Personal Computers:** The introduction of personal computers in the 1980s and 1990s revolutionized business automation by bringing computing power directly to individual employees.

   Software applications such as word processors, spreadsheets, and email clients enabled businesses to automate a wide range of tasks, from document creation to communication and collaboration.

6. **Internet and e-commerce:** The widespread adoption of the internet in the late 20th century further transformed business automation.

   E-commerce platforms, online marketplaces, and digital payment systems revolutionized the way businesses buy & sell goods/services, automating processes such as order processing, inventory management and customer service.

7. **Cloud Computing and SaaS:** In the 21st century, cloud computing and software-as-a-service (SaaS) models have made business automation more accessible and affordable for businesses of all sizes.

Cloud-based applications offer scalability, flexibility, and cost-effectiveness, allowing businesses to automate a wide range of processes without the need for expensive infrastructure or technical expertise.

8. **Artificial Intelligence and Robotics:** Recent advancements in artificial intelligence (AI) and robotics have opened up new possibilities for business automation.

   AI-powered algorithms can automate tasks such as data analysis, decision-making, and customer service, while robotics technology enables the automation of physical tasks in manufacturing, logistics, and other industries.

Understanding the fact of how fast the entire world changed through simple to complex automation, I want to ask you...

Isn't it time to automate your business so you can take out time for yourself, your spirituality, your family, your dreams, hobbies, and, most importantly, your future?

LET US UNDERSTAND HOW TO START!

The easiest way to automate a business, including a security alarms business in India, is to start with simple and readily available automation tools and gradually expand as needed.

STEP 1 - IDENTIFY MANUAL PROCESSES

Begin by identifying the manual tasks and processes that are repetitive and time-consuming in your business operations.

This could include tasks such as scheduling appointments, sending invoices, managing inventory, or responding to customer inquiries.

STEP 2 - CHOOSE AUTOMATION TOOLS

Research and select automation tools that are user-friendly, affordable, and suitable for your specific business needs.

There are many cloud-based software solutions available that cater to small businesses and offer features such as customer relationship management (CRM), accounting, project management, and marketing automation.

STEP 3 - IMPLEMENT BASIC AUTOMATION

Start by implementing basic automation for the identified manual processes.

For example, you can use scheduling software to automate appointment bookings, accounting software to automate invoicing and expense tracking, and email marketing software to automate customer communications.

Step 4 - Integrate Systems

Look for automation tools that offer integration capabilities to streamline your workflows further.

For instance, integrate your CRM system with your email marketing platform to automatically add new leads to your mailing list. This reduces manual data entry and ensures data consistency across systems.

Step 5 - Align Staff

First, conduct a team alignment meeting and get their consent to evolve together. Then provide training to and take feedback from the staff using the automation tools effectively.

Ensure they understand the benefits of automation and how it can improve their efficiency and productivity. Encourage them to embrace automation as a way to simplify their work and focus on more value-added tasks.

Step 6. Monitor and Evaluate

Regularly monitor the performance of your automated processes and gather feedback from your staff.

Identify any areas for improvement or additional automation opportunities. Be open to making adjustments and refinements as needed to optimize your automated workflows.

Step 7. Scale Gradually

As your business grows and evolves, gradually expand your automation efforts to cover more areas of your business operations.

c. Embrace CHANGE

Often in business, there are hard times that put us through stress, fear, and sometimes depression.

These negative feelings are something any progressive individual would want to get rid of almost instantly, whether they become self-conscious of them or encounter them externally. Trying to rid ourselves of these feelings can sometimes lead to desperation, prompting us to make decisions we later regret, such as choosing the wrong customer or offering a price lower than required, resulting in loss of revenue, time, effort, and ultimately, happiness.

To break this vicious cycle, I strongly recommend making a significant change. I urge all of our partners to consider and implement this change in the equation!

To change the game, we have to make some changes in our approach to playing. Let us understand what the above diagram is all about:

1. **Change in PRODUCT:** It is the simplest change in the equation, where we change the product that we are offering by identifying the product that our ideal customer really needs!
   - To achieve this, we have to meet our customers to identify their real needs and desires. Solving the unmet needs of our customers will not just help them but also

unlock a product or service which is really helpful for the society at large.

2. **Change in the DELIVERY:** Here everything remains the same, but the style or manner in which we deliver our products or services to the customer.

   For example, Netflix started as a DVD/CD rental company, then shifted to home deliveries, followed by an online DVD/CD rental service, and further evolved to become what it is today!

3. **Change in MARKET:** Working in a market which is not suitable for you will result in negative feelings. Sometimes, we have to identify a market that brings us happiness, where we are interested in doing business, that is a long-term market, is growing, and respects us as a product/service or solution provider. We have to constantly ask ourselves: Is the market suitable for me? Or Am I suitable for this market?

   While I can help you identify the market (geographically or psychologically) based on your real aspirations in due course, it requires careful thought as it involves stepping completely out of your 'comfort zone'.

4. **Change in YOU:** This is the easiest thing we can do! (Well, not really) but perhaps the most critical, controversial, and complex thing to change is to change YOURSELF.

   Since birth, we have become conscious and developed our likes, dislikes, thoughts, mindsets, and everything else!

   Changing the person may seem like an impossible task, but what we can change is how we do what we think we want to do.

In simpler terms, change the technique by adopting a new perspective. This may seem easy, isn't it?

While there can be thousands of tiny things, we can change in our style of doing what we do. The simplest of them to do as an entrepreneur is to change the style we SELL!

Want to know, how?

By **Conversational Selling!**

Let us dive deep into it... Conversational Selling is an approach to sales that focuses on engaging prospects in two-way, personalized conversations to understand their needs, address their concerns, and guide them through the buying process. It involves using natural language and communication channels such as live chat, messaging apps, social media, phone calls, or face-to-face interactions to facilitate meaningful dialogues with potential customers.

How to achieve this skill?

1. **Personalization**

   Tailoring the conversation to the individual needs, preferences, and interests of the prospect. This may involve researching the prospect's background, understanding their pain points, and customizing the sales pitch accordingly.

2. **Active Listening**

   Actively listening to the prospect's responses, questions, and feedback to understand their perspective and uncover valuable insights. This helps build rapport, demonstrate empathy, and address objections effectively.

3. **Asking Open-Ended Questions**

   Asking open-ended questions that encourage the prospect to share more information about their challenges, goals, and preferences.

4. **Providing Value**

   Offering valuable insights, advice, or resources that help the prospect make informed decisions and solve their problems. Just like you would do with your best friend.

5. **Educating and Informing**

   Educating the prospect about the product or service features, benefits, and use cases in a clear and understandable manner. This helps build credibility and confidence in the offering.

6. **Building Relationships**

   Focusing on building long-term relationships with prospects based on trust, transparency, and mutual respect. This involves nurturing leads over time, staying in touch, and providing ongoing support even after the sale is closed.

7. **Closing the Sale**

   Guiding the prospect through the buying process and overcoming any objections or hesitations they may have. This involves demonstrating value, addressing concerns, and providing reassurance to facilitate a smooth and successful transaction.

Ready, Steady, Go – How you can leverage the steady source of revenue.

CHAPTER 4

TOWARDS THE BRIGHTER SIDE

1. Getting Ready for The Future!

Often, we visit astrologers, Pandits, or Tarot card readers looking for a sneak peak into the future...

What if I give you a glimpse of the future of the Security Alarms Industry?

Entering into the beautiful world of Security Alarms, knowing what is going to happen will help you make better and informed decisions. Let me make you see through the blurred lines into the future...

Imagine yourself waking up to a house of the future. A beautiful voice of your loved one waking you up with cute words expressing their love for you. You wake up and get ready. Fast forward, you suddenly get a call from your boss to catch the next flight to another city.

You don't have time to sort out things, so you simply open an app on your palm, smilingly telling the AI interface to guard your house while you're away for a couple of days. It acknowledges your desire and confirms.

You fly off to the destination, and meanwhile, some mischievous individuals come by your house while you're gone. But guess what? As soon as they try to enter your premises, a loud siren goes off, and within seconds, a voice of a person warns them to get out of the premises. However, since they know this is a routine affair for automatic systems, they pay no heed to the voices and continue breaking into your house. Since security & crime go hand in hand, within seconds, a licensed drone equipped with pepper spray and white smoke gas is deployed, scaring off the intruders.

While all this may seem like a scene from a sci-fi movie, it is soon going to be a reality.

If you believe you would want to ride the bus to the future of Integrated command and control, contact our team for additional information on how to set up your own Integrated Command & Control center in India.

2. **What The FUTURE Holds – Forecasting & Predicting the Future of Alarms**

The advancement of technology has unlocked a bright future for anyone in the business of technology. The security alarm industry is also set to benefit from this advancement in tech, particularly in terms of AI, ML, internet of things, and cohesive & integrated systems.

While too much technology is often a risk, just the right amount of technology can help reduce the risk while offering the same practical benefits.

As per reports from leading market research companies, the security alarm industry is set to grow into a multi-million-dollar industry by 2030.

There are people of all mindset, needs, desires and so there are some with criminal intent. According to forecasts of crime statistics, crime does not seem to come down anytime soon.

Being in the business of security, it is a noble duty to help clients or people from society feel safe and lead a happy & healthy life. In order to safeguard them from crimes, the need for a security alarm system integrated with other security gadgets and even monitored by a specialized team is the future.

As a security professional, you are aware of the risks of the future, and one of the great answers to the problems of the future is a rapid action solution rather than a post-mortem tool!

One must look out for the superior technologies of the future (some of these have already been implemented in many countries):

1. Integrated command center for neighborhoods/residential complexes
2. DIY security alarm system integrated with locks
3. IoT security sensors working with your home automation system automatically
4. AI-powered remote command & control room with Quick Response Team
5. Integrated vehicle, home, business security suite
6. Integrated platforms with cybersecurity for smart services

The future of alarms is promising and in line with the advancement of the technology of the world!

Think about creating a business that works for generations to come, spanning throughout the country, in different business verticals... imagine yourself as the top management leading this amazing business and helping the world become a better place.

If you were able to imagine this, how would you feel?

WHAT TO DO NEXT?

By now, you must have received some actionable value which, if deployed well, can offer you massive revenue in your current business and unlock doors of the new world as we see it.

From our view, the security alarm business offers a steady source of revenue through AMC contracts and makes sure you get more value from your customers not only in monetary terms but in the form of respect, happiness, and positivity.

Anyone with the passion to grow can easily achieve success in this business. As entrepreneurs, our job is not just to sell, but to create an environment for our clients to buy and to assist them in making informed decisions.

For this, we need to have comprehensive knowledge not only of our products/services but also of our customers' world - their threats, mindsets, fears, frustrations, and desires.

With this knowledge, we can win the heart of our customer, gain true friendship, and achieve the ultimate goal of BE-ING USEFUL

I believe books are an amazing way to share, but there is one constraint – page limits! I hate page limits as much as you do because there is so much more, I want to offer you, but thankfully, I have a hack for that too...

If you want to know more about any of the chapters or the topics I have covered, join our Digitals WhatsApp Channel using the following link:

However, if you have urgent requirements and feel that a brief call would be ideal to address your query, remember, I am just a call away.

To schedule a call with me or with any of our experts, you can always drop us an email at ***di.corp@digitalsindia.com***, and we will get in touch with you to schedule a short meeting to address and help you in the best manner.

It is amazing that we have another GUARDIAN for this world, and the world will be a better & safer place for all!

A lot of gratitude towards you!

And remember, at Digitals, we are committed to providing top-notch security solutions tailored to your needs, ensuring your peace of mind.

Saksham Rajwanshi
DIGITALS INDIA SECURITY PRODUCTS PVT. LTD. .